THE CARDINALS

Amy Speace

© 2024, Amy Speace
All Rights Reserved

I couldn't have written this book without the help of my mentors Douglas Manuel and Maggie Smith and the faculty of the Naslun-Mann MFA in Creative Writing at Spalding University.

This book is dedicated to my grandmother, Rosalie A. Davis, who taught me my lifelong love of words and always told me life is richer if you read Proust in the original French, which I never did.

Photos by Jamey Wood

Contents

ONE

The Cardinals	9
Cumberland	10
On the day you left me,	11
The Fifth of July	13
Improvisation	14
East Nashville, 2022	16
Impatience	19
Drake's Creek at Dusk	20
Separation	22
Carousel	23
Tornado	24
Storm Warning	25
How to Drive in a Snowstorm	26
Consignment	27
Marriage	29
Arguing with Divinity	30

TWO

Sacraments	32
Night Shift	37
The Dresser	38
Baltimore 1968	39
Origin Story	40
Alexine	42
Constellations	43
To my Sister, Again and Again	44
The Gift	45
Super 8	46
Excavation	48

THREE

Tennessee Sweetgrass	50
Covenant	51
Saudade	52
As the Ball Drops on New Year's Eve in Two Time Zones	53
Truth, North Carolina	54
Tumbleweeds	56
Between the Rincons and the Catalinas	57
Moon River	58
Veterans Day	59
Forecast	60
Dinosaurs	61
Mothership	62
Egg Donor #2346	63
Caesura	65
Haiku: Apostasy	66
On The Anniversary Of Sedition,	68
Annica	70

ONE

The Cardinals

Everywhere when
        I'm not looking,

nowhere when I beg,
        a magic trick, I call

to my father, now dead,
        who said he would return

red. You'd think they'd sing
        for all their beauty,

but they click and squawk
        without song, like nothing

special, morning birds,
        everywhere, nowhere,

lifting their wings, two
        by two, one bright

and ordinary, the other dull
        and grey as February.

Cumberland

I often pass along the waterway and leave
    the thoughts that eddy alone.
        Deer crunch pine and plastic bags full

of excrement. I am a liar if I say I believe all
    is possible. You weren't. Always birds in pairs
        appearing every day along the trail. They tease

me with meaning. The shallows swell with broken feathers and
    sheer voile of ragweed sheen, a film that reflects
        the moaning bridge. No such thing

as answered prayers, only bark that curls and falls,
    following the river curving Kentucky's highland grasses, then
        crossing into Tennessee and back again, holding on

to something slippery that doesn't want to be held.

On the day you left me,

*Even when it's I who am escaped from,
I am half on the side of the leaver.*
                    —Sharon Olds, "Stag's Leap"

I reluctantly signed the papers as rain
slapped on the slack roof and
the little lawyer with her smoker's voice
said, *I'm sorry,* as she'd probably
said many times that day.

On the day you left me, I floated as if
it were temporary, this time
being lost in a cavern, a dark
honeypot, dripping sweet fingers
to be smeared over the crest
of a kiss that crashed and
crashed and crashed and
you said,
one of us will have to move out,
so even
though it was me
who left, we
both knew it was you.
I wanted
to be the one
to show contrition.
I didn't like our house
like I liked our home.
.
I moved and moved and
moved again, each time taking
more furniture, framed photos of
our son, a keyboard, the third guitar, my
books in stacks each time I'd stop
by, hoping to be invited into
our bed one more time rather than

sleep in a borrowed room without room
for my fugitive grief.

Nothing was mine anymore, mostly
you.

You spoke of *trying* or *hoping* but
They were flat noises, a moaning
of non-meaning, a lie, a lie,
a lie. I wanted you sleeping
next to me until the day I died.
I wanted your decrepit teeth, your
stink, your skinny old arms
around me. I wanted nothing more
than everything and there you were,
asking me to leave,
asking me to sign papers that cut
the chord I wrote over and over
in my head to try to sing us saved.

I wrote three love songs in my life.
They were all to you.
Now my innocence embarrasses me.

On the day you left me, I twirled
your ring on my fourth finger, grooving
it deeper into my skin as if that
would keep my feet on the ground.

The Fifth of July

A clearing of spinners, snakes and paper cups—

the aftermath celebration, the day of conception—
    nothing special to the sun.

I lay, legs spread
    on a hospital bed,

a tube inserted, plastic twine,
    catheter syringe. A beeping

from behind the window. We're ready,
    she said. In went the sparkler.

I brought no prayer, having steeled myself for failure.
    He was beside me, holding my hand,

a fistful of years before he dropped it
    finger by finger, again.

Improvisation

Having packed my survival
in two boxes, I carry
what he won't miss now

that I am gone—olives and cheese,
turmeric and bay leaves,
sheets of sea salt seaweed,

the love song I wrote behind walls
we built from years of wishing.
I have one day to resettle

into a temporary cabin, exposed
beams, cold floors, cracked
concrete, Persian rugs, askew.

The first thing I miss
is my piano. The second—we
were stuck inside for a year. Now

I am stuck outside for a week,
or a month, or—. Here, children sled
down lanes on cookie sheets, on thin

aluminum, crusted by cookies, cooked
by a mother with nothing to grieve.
Here, Hackberries hang

to the cliff overlooking
the Cumberland, wide and unsettled,
with crossing currents, a river

I met just a few years before.
Here, is not my home. This is not
my key. Here is a scale I am trying

to hear, a melody so foreign.
Notes inside notes inside notes.
After all these years,

my fingers remember:
forgiveness, repair—
the only scale I know to sing,
the only place I know to begin.
East Nashville, 2022

East Nashville, 2022

1.

My son loves to push from underneath the green
froth at the Margaret Maddox YMCA on Gallatin Pike,
splashing the father who is gently introducing

his baby to chlorine and crowds, theirs—the only
skin of color in this beryl water. I catch
myself, staring at the boy

and his father, aware—
too aware of my cold nipples, skinny
pocked thighs, the whiteness of my

C-section belly, swollen years after
        the cut, always hidden from the sun.

2.

My mother told me stories of segregated pools
growing up in Baltimore, a Catholic city where
I was born three months before Martin Luther King
was shot. The town blazed that April with Molotov cocktails
and rage. We lived in the quiet of the country, with no idea
of what was burning downtown. She uses blackness
as a descriptor, leaving whiteness out as if assumed, as in,
the other day a BLACK woman... or *the other day a woman....*

3.

We married
in this home
in this
neighborhood.
He moved
to the west
side of town,
far from the changes
in the east, where

I remain. He doesn't like
change, although he
changed everything. We
were separated, separate.
He took off
the ring. I looked.

4.

East Nashville is Hair Worlds,
the Diesel College, Dollar Marts

and check-cashing stores, ten-dollar
coffees served by blonde-bearded boys,

overcharging parking lots,
graffitied metro bus stops, white

brick walls beaming with Opry legends.
Hushed tones of one-sided gentrification, far

from the neighborhood it used to be
when the west side called it the "DMZ,"

but never knew of that crooked tree where,
occasionally, a red flag would fly, indicating

the smoker was on as an invitation, bbq in the backyard,
$5.00 for a pork sandwich with sweet beans and tart slaw.

In my neighborhood, red brick ranchers
are painted white with black shutters before

being sold to transplants from California.
Developers buy on the cheap, tear down

middle-class homes where entire
generations were raised in order to build

four tinderboxes on one plot for triple the sale.
They've torn down the meat-and-three

for Asian Fusion and Bubble Tea.
Something lost, something gained,

they say.

5.

I am flailing as a single mother.

6.

Back to the Y, back to the water, where
the boys slap the blue side by side, separated
by the buoy marker. I sit alone on the edge,

feet dipped into the steaming cold rather than enter
the shivering. The father plays in the pool with his son.
My Pisces son loves to swim and jump and doesn't ask

me about the Black of the boy in the pool
       next to him.

Impatience

The bird, who doesn't know reflection, flies
directly into the window in front of my desk, where I

sit writing (or not) every day. The grey
presses down the ink, but I only see the green

of the buds of the Hackberry limbs, reaching
toward March. The suicide bird keeps

barging at the light, head down, a battering
ram. Does she see her reflection

or mine? Crashing the glass, does she dream,
like me, that time will explode, cutting

through the screened divider? Or does she not
think at all, birds being birds—little

Icarus, unaware of the danger of
pushing too hard toward the light.

Drake's Creek at Dusk

The heron stands on one leg,
    the other, a sideways A, which,

once I say
    an *A*, our son mimes

lines in the air: one down,
    then up, then

the bridge.
    He calls it that.

But, my love, you said
    redemption, and I knew

it was yours you spoke,
    not mine, not ours. I'm being

a stickler, but not
    to our son, who really

mimed an *H*.
    But who should tell him

this? Not I, as I
    stand on these pebbles,

watching the bird
    balance on her pestle,

resting on the rock in the middle
    of the pond that pours

into the lake, waiting,
    perhaps. How can I know

if we ever were a *we*,
        and would knowing repair

the rippling tear
        like the lines that may not

touch, no matter
        the attempt of the child

who is just there
        making an *H* or an *A*, watching

the bird in the middle
        of the pond that feeds

into the lake as patient
        as redemption.

Separation

Smooth yellow yarn,
red cedar arms. Here

in the dusty vintage aisles, musty
with grass-stained silver, scalloped

silk tap pants, board games worn
umber at the edge, and chairs

like the one sleeping at the top
of the stairs with the handwritten

"Artisan $150"—
                    as if a chair
could stitch us back together.

Carousel

Nashville, March 27, 2023

I hold his hand too tightly. He asks
for cotton candy. This time I say,

yes. He asks for popcorn. This time
I say, *yes*. We linger

near the monkeys, *hoo hooing*,
not caring how loud we are.

We run to the carousel so he can get
the frog this time. I ride up

and down on an antelope next to him,
the late afternoon light a stain

on his cheek. He goes up. I go down. He says,
Mama you're riding the cantaloupe!

He says, *Mama, look at us going in circles*!

I go wherever he wants.
Hotdogs for dinner. I buy him

whatever he wants at the store.
He chooses a stuffed Pterodactyl, names it

Terry. I hold him too tight. He says, *Mama
I can't breathe*,

and I squeeze his body close enough
to fold him into my soft belly as if

I can put him back where
he entered this wounded world.

Tornado

In the dark, in a bathtub
at the center of the house,
flashlight, pillows, blankets,
boots, just in case. Sirens
scream. My phone slams
warnings over and over.
We two are alone.
My son sleeps
through the horns,
the strap of his bike helmet
under his nose. Before
his eyes flutter shut,
he asks about the potato
coming, mispronouncing
the storm. I do my best
to make up a song to shush
him to slumber in my arms,
ready to throw my back
against the shards,
my breakwater body.
The dog is somewhere
under a bed. The hail
shoots buckshot at
the glass. *Take shelter
in your safe space*, the phone
blinks a warning, and I think,
here in this bathtub, awaiting
the wind, I am more
sheltered and safe,
my baby to breast, than I
have been in a long year waiting
for my marriage to end.

Storm Warning

A friend of mine once told me
of a dead horse he drove past
in a frozen field. It lay
on its side, sliced stem to stern,

guts splayed on wheat. He said,
*That would make a great dead horse
trampoline*, as if there was such a thing.
I said, *Is there no mystery left?*

I wonder about earthquakes,
How you'd ever not expect
the ground to rive beneath you
after swaying with the ripple

of rock and sediment, feet far
apart, bracing for the worst.
45,000 is a small city. People
buried under concrete,

not a fleeting thought or a
wondering. I left
last week before the tornado
warnings. It is late

winter. Three years ago one
ripped Holly Street in half--
guts of houses, kindling confetti,
winter carcasses left to rot.

How to Drive in a Snowstorm

Look, it takes balls to weather this
storm when others stay off the roads, those
who think they know weather. The cowards
nestle on cracked couches under crochet
wool, kids home from school, restless,
wrestling on braided oval rugs strewn
with pudding spoons while a mother waits
at the window for her husband's car. Or,
in another house, new lovers lay on another
rug watching porn, the novelty of
being iced in together. Hazards on. Slow.
Don't tell me I don't know.
Wipers crusted, a smear
on glass slides a blur
at eye level, so you have to drive slumped
to see under the iced arc, squinting slush.
Blast the heat just on knees and feet
as the defrost on high fogs the window.
I'll never figured that one out.
Don't tell me how to drive through this
Nor'easter. I've been here before,
when I fled after my first
marriage crumbled into driveway gravel.
Ignore the text buzz. Flat
flakes bat the wind like a kitten hit them.
This is how you drive
in a snowstorm
in an economy rental
as light as the frost of leaving.

Consignment

Racks of little clothes on little
      white hangers, *6 mos 9 mos 18 mos 24 mos,*
           stretching the time, size by size.

The longest days, the shortest year,
      they say. I skip to the 4Ts, two
           racks away. Nothing here

but T Rex t-shirts, out-of-season shorts
      and swim trunks. The treasures hide
           in the outer aisle. $20

Pottery Barn toolkit -- hammer, wrench, nails.
      Paw Patrol desk and chair -- perfect! –
           $15, a small stain on the top

from a marker or paint. No matter!
      Tedious rectangular tables
           lined up like teeth,

and underneath, bins of "Toddler Toys!",
      claps the handwritten sign where
           excavators and fire engines tangle

lifts and ladders. Lightening McQueen
      everything. My son is on his knees
           in a food truck, punching

cash register numbers that sing and ring,
      assembling plastic pizzas and tacos
           for my lunch. I haul a basket

full of books and toys, shorts for spring,
      Kentucky blue Nike sneakers to replace
           the ones he outgrew this winter.

Those, I choose for my husband.
    I just texted him. *Do you need*
        anything? He would not

have texted me. *I found him*
    a new pair of blue sneakers ☺
        Thanks, he typed, no punctuation.

I surround myself with second-hand
    clothes, consigned to the February cold.
        World without end.

Marriage

A cock and a hen
stand stooped, back

to back clucking
at pale pebbles

of grain, each
like the bobbing

bird at desktops
littered with legal

briefs, piles of
ins, stacks of

outs, as the
yellow plastic

beak picks at
pens, paperclips,

sharpener. Back
to the birds,

at odds with
the facts. Eating

their fill. Not
seeing each other.

Arguing with Divinity

This morning, my son took
my face between
his hands and said, *Mama,
you are lovely.*
I thought of the planet
Venus, its coiling,
gaseous clouds and shrinking
storm, and that my son says
it is his favorite planet,
merciless shivery,
like the star sand
that winks at his
face when turned to
evensong.

      In the end
we will be mantle and core,
nuttall and mud, and pairs
of common cardinals
caught in foaming churn,
helium heave, light years
from our litanies,
fire blinking desires
from a distance too far.

TWO

Sacraments

1.

The first time
I heard the word
cunt
it was the flash
of my mother's
that I saw between
that c and t—
the *un*
like a shrug.
Such a little word—
a canyon.
Once, tucking
me in at night, the
peach robe slipped
open and, as she
bent over—
a coil.
I saw the curl
and looked away—
a constellation,
the danger—
a consecration
of devotion.

2.

My first period dripped during a Girl Scout camping trip
led by lesbians before I knew that word. They gave me an OB
and told me I'd lost my cherry.

I remember the feel of blood, as I pushed
the small cotton stub inside the folds of my skin.
I like the poetry of the monthly shedding of useless

feathers, and still welcome the grip
of the maiden at my lower back, even as I prepare
for the end of migration.

3.

When I was 25, my mother sent me home
to Brooklyn while I was having a miscarriage

in Delaware, where my family was vacationing, as we had
my whole life. One morning, I sat on the sunrise sand.

The cramps kicked, a tearing from inside,
weeks before the waffling sentence of ruling. It took

everything I had to tell her of the blood, to ask
what to do. She packed me a coke and sandwich,

her eyes swimming with regret. She whispered, *I'm sorry,
but this would kill your father.*

I drove north for five hours on I-95 in standstill
Saturday traffic, from Rehoboth to Cobble Hill where,

in a used Honda Prelude, broken air conditioning,
I bled out a baby while drinking a warm soda.

For years I smiled through false forgiveness
when the truth was hot fire, a tornado, a lion,

not enough wine. But if I stare hard enough
at that peach silk – a robe with matching sash,

matching gown, matching my mother's knees
when she'd kneel next to me on the fading

yellow shag rug on Maplewood Lane off Route 99
across from the corn and sunken graves—if I stare

hard enough at my mother to see her as a child
surrounded by rosary widows praying the Hail Mary,

I can see her full of grace—*blessed art thou*—
Women—fruit of thy womb—while I

sit by, reading a book, the perfume of my mother's
desires wrapping around me from her open robe.

4.

Mother is a country, a little land
in the middle of the ocean where the edge
of the sand is swallowed by a dream,

Mother is an island in the Milky Way,
sleepwalking the swell of the waves
up and down and floating out to sea.

Mother is a pebble pile of glass and shell,
under slippery curve of rock,
making a nest of stars and fallen leaves.

No one hears the prayers she sings,
lost in the moss of moonlight,
nightly watches spent on rocking knees.

Lu la lee, hush now baby don't you weep
Close your eyes I'll rock you back to sleep

Mother is a country where tidepools
fill when gravity calls the sun and moon
to take their place in line.

Peace was made with the storms that came,
arms were laid at the foot of the harbor,
a betting on the wrecking ball of night.

Lu la lee…

The needle drips and the voices blur,
the pull of bones and he slips to earth.
She knows she'll grieve the separating life.
She knows she'll grieve the separating life.

5.

My son won't remember you, Mother.
He balances on a flat stone in the middle
of the brook rippling over red pebbles.

We carry plastic candles with battery lights,
scraps of paper with your last words,
bits of you we have held onto these two years.

We scatter your ashes at the edge
of the creek at the bottom
of the hill in the woods where Dad

built the log cabin of your childhood
dreams. The priest thumbed your head
like a sacrament, even though you held

onto your protest through the end.
You weren't right about everything.
You were right about everything.

These trails cut and marked
with flags and paint, wind from
runnel to ridge. I hiked here to heal.

The day after a Thanksgiving, you
made me buy a mattress. You said,
if you buy a bed, you will leave him.

I left, that
mattress, a bedframe—all
that I took.

Sisters and brothers, on either side
of the water, my son in my arms. Someone
has a speech prepared. We share

 a story. Our stories don't match.
We argue the facts, exiled
by details. A confession

of grief, each to our own. Each
in our own version of the story,
each our own sovereign country.

Night Shift

My mother would throw open the curtains of our darkened
yellow room singing, *O what a beautiful morning!*, the stabbing
sun at high noon, a cheery scold as the house had been

moving for hours, alive as a corporation. *I never saw the sunrise until
I had a baby and then I saw every hour.* At night she'd dress in her
bridal peach nightgown, long gauze train, satin straps holding her
to her vow, over sweatpants smeared with flour handprints. Curled
under covers, my sister and I would squeal when she'd enter our room.
She called herself the night nymph and would dance us off to sleep,
while our father worked past dinner, past stories, past dreaming.

The Dresser

My mother's shame
is not my own
under her peach satin gown,
folded in the thin top drawer,
mahogany and brass.
I'd take it out and try it on
in front of the floor-length mirror.
The other: blue, bridal lace.
The peach smelled most like her,
a Jean-Nate talcum mist
that floated on the top
From a sachet made of lavender,
fragile as a music box.

My father's side
was on the right,
which seems correct
and true,
the opposite
of Mother's gowns—
quarters, matches, keys,
a Boy Scout pin, Eagle Scout,
Bible with flaking initials
held together by rubber bands
to keep the years from spilling.
I stole coins and matches just to see
if he would notice me at all.

Baltimore 1968

My mother's lace gloves on the White's Only fountain
just down from the spice factory, blocks from where, on
February 8, I was born at Baltimore General,
south of the Mason, north of the Dixon,
an in-between place of civil accents.

A rowhouse town boarded, a rotted harbor of ignorance,
shuttered and sheltered, one side of the tracks.
In April the riots broke out for the King
two months after my christening in an antique white dress.

My mother, a native, her city scented
with cinnamon and tea that kited the sky,
like the Molotov cocktails arcing above Washington's
pinnacle just down from the McCormack spice factory.

Take my hand, precious lord, and play it pretty,
Martin Luther asked Ben, the organist, the night before
he died. Half of the city took to the streets
and sang Hallelujah through fury and fire.

Baltimore smelled like high tea at Hecht's
at the top floor of the fading department store
where my grandmother took me to eat cucumber sandwiches,
where black waiters with white gloves never looked at me once.

Origin Story

She taught me how to read
by putting letters together
on road signs. On her lap
in the days before strapping
children in the back. I don't
remember this. I was three.
By the time I was five,
she bought me the *Annotated
Alice in Wonderland* that sits
next to my bed. The last book
she read was *Love in the Time
of Cholera*, which she didn't like
because of the sex scenes.

She taught me how
to read. She wore white
gloves to church, boiled wool
dresses, sensible shoes,
stockings that drooped
at her ankles. She memorized
poetry and carried change
for the homeless in her clasped
clutch, hanging on her wrist.
She smelled of Jean Nate
and rose talcum. She rubbed my
back with alcohol and powder
singing "Beautiful Dreamer."
The kitchen smelled of
the white gas oven.
Violets on the windowsill
in little cups. She said, *Be a lady*
and things like that,
a foreign language.
I liked to swear
and do the opposite.
She never remarried

and her last words were *Bob,*
I'm coming home. May be a myth
but I believe it. She was the closest
to God I've known.

                      She taught
me how to read.

Alexine

My niece, five, watches me
with eyes wider than the flying

range of the gull who lands
on undulating sands.

I tell her of the magic—
raging seas on fabric

no thicker than her hair,
sea-light and barely air.

She asks me of the stars—
dark cannot swallow it all—

I tell her there's an art
to the wishing

Constellations

I am older by a year. I have words,
dresses, the big bed. She stays
small in the child's bed. The door

is thin. I can hear the party, clinking
glasses, laughter. I am claustrophobic
behind the closed door. She is asleep.

The door opens with a squack. One
of my father's salesmen—later I will remember
his name as Mike—comes

through the door, over to my big girl bed
and leans down, bourbon breath
near my cheek. He stumbles,

kisses my lips. My eyes are closed.
I am still and silent. He tiptoes out.
I open my eyes to the dark, lit

by the glow in the dark stars that twinkle
their patterns of hunters at the head
of the short bed where my sister sleeps, my sister,

who will never know this
memory my parents will deny
when, decades later, I finally remember.

To my Sister, Again and Again

A smearing summer
aftermath of black

berries on the wagontop,
before August bows out.

You keep pushing me
out of the summers

we shared. Hackberries
loom and spit their cud

in hard crusted heaps.
Your silence shutters.

It is hard to clean the stick
off the car, in the direct

line of fire, as I feel
every time you don't answer.

The Gift

He sinks into his worn
        recliner, hooked to

a clicking machine,
        pumping his breath through

hoses attached to his nose.
        The morphine steals everything.

My small son is in his lap.
        He makes a ceremony

of gifting his dog-eared
        Bible, a pocket watch, and

a wooden box painted by
        a long-forgotten lover:

two beech trees and boxing gloves.
        He stories his past to a child

who will not remember his face. I will
        hold these things in a bedside drawer

behind books, lavender, frankincense.
        Then, a half smile pulled his skin,

and the first of October's moaning
        shook the sergeant leaves.

Super 8

There is a super 8 film—
    the Badlands—
        a silhouette
           of a girl
on top of a peak,
    knees drawn,
        stubbornly waiting
           on rescue.
              Cut.
A Buick station wagon window,
    the camera pointing
        at the girl, fading
           in reverse angle,
dissolving, less and
    less until she is just
        a dot and the filmstrip
           explodes
with emulsion and light,
    silver halide
        crystals of salt
           suspended in gelatin.
Numbers and dots. Then the film flaps
    its wings, a playing
        card in bike spokes.
           The end. White screen.
              Cut.
There is a super 8 film
    a father narrates at parties,
        voicing the part of the daughter
who is sitting on the peak, knees drawn,
    as the car pulls away, leaving her.
        A prank played on the 8-year old
who sits in the back of the room still
    sucking her thumb at 16, listening to the father
        suck the wind out of the room.
In 24 frames anyone can see

                The loneliness of the plains
                            In 50 feet of Kodachrome.
                                            Cut.
There is a super 8 film
            disintegrating
                        in a metal file tucked
                                    in the back
of a closet. The girl
            will throw away the film
                        and, on the 2nd Tuesday of the month,
                                    the recycling truck will swallow it whole.

Excavation

Green sorbet tile. 2005. The color of a high school hallway.
Black and white linoleum floors. What I stared at.
Men and women holding signs, trying hard to change my mind.
Blood and bone. Numb. Alone.
$300 in cash to repair my cunt. The word
clinic is matter of fact. I took a cab and lied
about doing so. I told them he was coming
but there was no one coming.
Seagram's Ginger Ale and Lorna Doones—what I woke to,
little bit of sweet and fizz filling up the emptiness.
I think I wrote that somewhere else. I plagiarize myself.
Have I just lost the ability to describe that no
one gets here on a good day no matter what they later say?
That linoleum floor, those green walls, blood and bone
being sucked through a hose while I lay sleeping.

THREE

Tennessee Sweetgrass

Something is starting, you know.
        Something is starting, you

know, with bullhorns and drag queens
        stampeding the steeple, feet pounding

on marble, marching band time.
        Fronds folding in on mean

concrete in all neighborhoods, even
        the north side projects, shuttered

where beauty is seen in little miracles—
        hustle of shouts and signs,

a gathering southern storm,
        crowding the capital. Two elected

black men are singled
        out and censured, which was no surprise

to anyone. Hospitality is
        reserved for the seemingly

courteous, white folks, fearful of the shade—
        The light came in late afternoon

and threw colors across the marble
        ballasts. Order was restored.

For now. *Deus ex machina.*
        Sometimes hostility

hides at the level
        of the sweet summer grass

that bends over the path.

Covenant

I come to the page with hostility.

My mind is blank
as the blistered sky, too
much for this day—this
day—another that will fade
and fold and we will all
move onto other picturesque,
terrible days. The trees
preen their new blossoms,
forgetting that it's rude
to commit such selfishness
today.

Today is not for vanity.

Today is for the shattering
of bones, small bird
bones, impossibly broken
in a hallway. I come
to the page with a request:
do not let this be mediocre,
do not let me fall
into line, even though
I have nothing to say.

Saudade

The rain, pricks to remind—
winter still owns the sky. I am
lost in the cold clouds, worrying
my loosening jowls,
newly soft from the year of loss,
as if such a thing could be a gain.

January hits its target, the arrow
at its mark, just a bit off
center in the replay as the fog rolls in
again and again. I almost wrote
"aging" —it was a spell-check thing,
like capitalizations I have to correct.
Remember white out? I have
white out mornings, like when I woke with
sangria on my lips from that night, decades ago—
I slept with a man from Seia
whose name I never knew in a crowded
hostel just off the plaza, guitars
gut strung, playing past last call
(or so I thought in my headspun dreams).
Idealized danger is for the young, who wake
with glue crusted eyes. Like mine.
It's impossible to see with that shit
in the way of clarity.

The end of this month is a headache,
the month of the second anniversary
of the leaving and the first of the cleaving.
It dropped 70 degrees last week
in one day. One day. On Christmas,
I let the dog out in -2 degree windsharp.
I miss the days when the only decision
was which town, which train. I thought
escaping south, I'd find what the north
never offered. Mildness. Steadiness.

As the Ball Drops on New Year's Eve in Two Time Zones

O those nights of northern frost, holidays on Chesapeake,
    with sugar plums and sure belief, blind to what would soon

be lost. Now I lie at eventide where dogs dig
    in this sand for bones, and tidal spray sticks

in my throat. If I could, I'd stay awhile, let the clock sneak
    out the year. Stars could smear mistakes

like mine, blurring past and present lines. Again,
    a break I couldn't see. Instead of here where I hide

in black tie mistletoe charades, monotonous.

Truth, North Carolina

The green rectangle announced a single digit population
on Main Street. A white church steeple, straight
as a crane obscured by scaffolding.

The Post Office flag flew at half-mast for a stranger.

I had diverted to extend the journey, pondering
a pace, east of the highway (not a road
for rumination) to delay the unknown,

on the way home toward the things
we had collected. I took a photograph.
Stopped for lunch.

The coffeehouse waitress, pen poised above the pad,
leaned in to whisper of a payphone at the edge
of town on the Appalachian Trail

that phones the pizza parlor directly.
Charges are reversed at no cost to hikers
on their way to Georgia or Maine.

I lost track of time. Four o clock.
The sun was low. I left a tip.
Filled my tank. Turned north.

Three hundred miles. I'd have to choose—
A cheap motel?
A late night drive?

Just ahead another sign—"Luck"—a straight line down Main,
too close to not feel the brush with the divine.
Across this one, nailed to the metal, orange, askew—

"Luck Closed—Detour Left"

A joke, a prophesy, a poetry
of pilgrims centuries before
my hesitation home.

"Truth is always open for business,"
said a friend years later when I showed her
the faded photos found in a box,

the things I took before I left
to change my name.

Tumbleweeds

But I know, there is nothing
for me in tumbleweeds—
dry fingers of bonedust
across desert redrock scrub.
Odessa is an emptiness, the pain
at the edge of my chest.
When you drive west,
lightening sharpens
it's crack across the flats.
I follow the brake lights of the semi
into the storm. Radio is only
prattling preachers
and Tejano music, so I
choose the Gospel according
to West Texas.
I shouldn't have come.
I shouldn't have come.
Leaving is an art
I don't know.

Between the Rincons and the Catalinas

I sit crosslegged on a painted stone and settle
my breathing to a half state. It's here

I think the sky is showing off: pastel
crinoline and pink underthings,

thoroughbreds at the line, a soprano to the mic,
birds at the canyon poised before

the desert wakes. Prayer, a dream, sneaks
in with the dawn and dusk like a song.

Tell me, when did you know you stopped loving me?

The rabbit stands guard like a sentinel.
The dove perched on the Saguaro auditions.
The moon caught naked without a choice.

Moon River

I thought my son was too young to notice
        the absence of his father in the house.

the absence of me in the other. Maybe
        he needs me to dream next to him.

He asks for me to scratch his back while
        singing "Moon River." We're in my bed.

He hasn't wanted to sleep in his own
        for months. "Moon River"

was the first song I sang to him, hours old,
        on my breast, my husband watching

a basketball game on the hospital tv,
        although somehow he thought to catch

that moment on video. Tonight I sing
        "Moon River." My son rolls over

after one time through and lifts his arms
        for me to scratch and sing again.

Veterans Day

Today, Milton will be
in his dress blues, haunting
the Waffle House and Red Lobster. Vets
eat free. He doesn't want to be
thanked for his service.
The temperature dropped
twenty degrees today.
Snow predicted. Leaves
leave boughs. Kerry and his team
crunched piles into mulch
in my yard yesterday —yesterday,
the rain; today the sun. Hard
to predict the waver of grief.
Tonight, the moon will tease:
her dulled corner, lack of stars
and stripes waving
at the atmosphere.
If my son were here, he'd
hold his hands to the moon
to shield the light, zip up his jacket
as we walk the dog, barely aware
of the war.

Forecast

The light comes uninvited.
It was supposed to rain today.

I check, feeling for my phone, before
my eyes fully open.

Chance of thunderstorms, yet
here she is flaunting her flame

over the flaked leaves, un-raked
in piles left forlorn, children in the front yard.

It is never too late, they say.
I say winter hardens the feeble bract,

lying on an overlooked lawn, losing
its scales in the cracked soil.

Such an obnoxious surprise—
when there is nothing to do

but accept the unacceptable
sun in your eyes.

Dinosaurs

I once stood in the center
of the arches in a Utah park.
Cost me $20 to stay until dark.
I'd pay it again and again

and again—a toll
for entering the fossil.

What have we become?
Beasts, bullets, the timing of
ballet in a box, gold
stalactites, small talk.

Where did you go? Where
are you going? My son, my son
sat up suddenly last
night in my bed, screaming

war and that his blanky was stolen
by dinosaurs.

Mothership

Sitting in front of "A Disaster At Sea" by Joseph Mallord Turner at The Tate Museum in London, while 7 months pregnant

The weight of constant grieving—
there is a heaviness to this—
the mother and child
at the center of the canvas.

There is a heaviness to this
as waves heave over the wreck.
At the center of the canvas
two heads bow together.

Waves heave, but here—
a cape of air—can you see?
Two heads together, bowing,
mother breathing to child.

A cape of air—
this is all I can see,
the weight of grieving,
constantly.

Is this all I can see anymore,
the constant grieving of holding
this weight, like a cape
of air?

All I can see anymore,
while I sit here rocking,
the weight of you. You
will be my howling kiss.

Child, I am mother—
at the center—
there is a heaviness
to the weight of constant grieving.

Egg Donor #2346

I stare at the photo and there
you are, your eyes, her
eyes, not mine. People say,

he has your eyes.
I chose her because
her eyes were green and wide like

mine, my sister's,
my mother's. There she is
smiling, her hand

in motion at the bob
of her beachcomber hair.
Your hair. You, half

made of a stranger. I think of her
gift and the probability
she needed our money.

Early one sunrise, rocking
in third trimester vigil,
laptop on my lap, I opened

the file, again, with you
in me when you were only
mine. Later, I thought *why*

look again at her when you're in
my lap on my breast? Mother
is me, the only name

that means anything
anymore. Now,
I latch my heart so far

inside that neither you
nor I, will erase my eyes.
The one photo I have of her

is inside a file inside a file
inside a file I may never find,
which was intentional.

Caesura

Tiny waterfalls, hormonal shifts,
    bloom dripping tingles
        across flesh, a spring hurling over a pebble,

hot house flowers across the scalp.
    This is not a caesura, this is a cessation,
        and who isn't afraid to say that, rather

than say it all may begin again. I know
    it won't. There is one shot here in this life
        to say the thing that needs be said,

to catch the follicle
    at its prime. To bleed
        on time. Or to not bleed.

The broom sweeps across the linoleum
    of the kitchen floor, catching the cuttings
        of hair from the child,

a shedding of itself, skin, follicles, drapery,
    holding off the too bright light
        from over the fallow field

once lined with corn, gravestones half sunk in the husk
    of the earth leaving half eulogies
        from centuries before.

Haiku: Apostasy

June

The heat breathes a hum
I am moored in this hulled house
No matter the mourn

He comes this morning
I am working on my heart
A blue hummingbird

July

The crickets demand
attention with their wheezing
I woke without you

The woodpecker digs
For morning fruit in the palm
My waiting heart

August

The sun spreads her arms
Around the eastern mountains
I had to apologize first

The first of the roosters
Asks permission of the dawn
I hold my breath

September

The smokers
Meditate each drag
In humble laughter

The morning old dove
Adds to the warm-up chord
I am close to forgetting you

On The Anniversary Of Sedition,

I drive my son to
daycare listening to the commentators
on the commission and censure,
interviewing senators who stitch
language like crosshatch on
motel wall décor.

Across the street, the neighbors
keep up their election signs
like an argument. I can see from here
they have two front doors, side
by side. One is white, like every other
front door on the block, a knocker, a peering
window; the other, an irrational
open space, a beggarly blue tarp,
casually tacked up at the top but left to
flap the bottom. They staked the oversized
blue flag yesterday, again,
in case we missed the semaphore.

I'd like to think
behind that tarp is a space
heater for the linoleum foyer,
cat piss, sweat of a life
held together by spit and prayer,
not enough to fix the door
but enough to get them through
the winter. They'll hold out long enough
to sell in the high market, roll west
to where they can rest away from
the neighborhood carpetbaggers who stole
their voices and who'd have, eventually,
come for their guns. I've settled

across the street from the stillness
still wondering who will be held

to the windblown weather
now that all is undone.
But the neighborhood hawk,
who has always been here,
stretches a shadow
over the snow like she knows
the end of the story.

Annica

I walked the river trail today. Again.
    An indigo bunting perched on
        the hackberry's witch limbs,

deep blue, as if Van Gogh himself
    had taken his brush to its wing. Why
        do the males own color

and song, defending their territory of desire?
    The grey drake carves into
        the viscous green sheen

that coats the pond, while turtles sun
    on broken limbs. I have loved.
        As well, I have learned.

I walk in rhythm to traffic
    and trains, meditating on how love
        ever survives this new normal

heat, blistering the water.
    Maybe I made it up,
        the mythos of ordinary birds.

I see no red
    of my cardinal today. Only
        the dull grey of the female,

waiting on melody and union.
    Annica. After all this time,
        I still don't know and maybe

that is the point. Keep
    your magic, *dukka*. Sweat
        drips down my shorts,

trailing the scar of my son.
      The bunting sings his song,
           learned in the womb.

He and I take stock of ordinary
      blessings. To be in love as love
           changes, as everything will.

Made in the USA
Columbia, SC
20 August 2024